praise for emily corwin

"Emily Corwin's exquisite new collection *tenderling* makes contemporary the truest traditions of myths and fairy tales—the ones filled with decadence and magic, the ones that find humor in blood and clarity in the surreal. In Corwin's poems, every skeleton has a vain side and there are sharp edges on all of the diaphanous shadows. There is sparkle in this collection, too, and Gurlesque wonder in ribbons and thorns, all of which helps us to break apart the modern performances of gender. Corwin makes it possible to dress up as hero, villain, or neither without losing the taste for lace and flowers. With these capacious and surprising poems, Corwin has created a full-color, fur-lined fairy tale for the 21st century." —Adrian Matejka, author of *Map to the Stars*

"Emily Corwin's *tenderling* is a luminous, bizarre, gorgeously racketed, rollicking, and sometimes terrifying radiance of poems. One after the next Corwin contorts diction and syntax and sense and story until you realize she has imagined and crafted an entire world—a world strange and haunted and sensuous. Beckoning and scary. Mythical and common at once. This is a remarkable book." —Ross Gay, author of *Catalog of Unabashed Gratitude*

"When the cutie-pie was opened, the birds began to sing, and what they sand was glittery and savage and fearless and dangerous—be careful with this book." —Cathy Wagner, author of *Nervous Device*

"Confronting and darling, every word a perfect warm circlet of pink blood, My Tall Handsome raids every crystal jar on the lace-topped vanity for truth, poison, and song until you can't remember why you ever thought pretty was better than powerful, sugar was better than bitter medicine, or dancing needed more music than your own voice." —Brain Mill Press

"Emily Corwin's interconnected collection of poetry is the dark side of a fairy tale. It's buttons made from bone on a wedding dress. It's ice cream with sauce, but that's not strawberry, it's blood. The beautiful language of this collection bangs through my head on a regular basis, the imagery so solid that you can almost touch the crabapple trees. Hands down the best poetry collection I read this year." —Kolleen Carney, Zoetic Press

acknowledgments

Day One, "anxiety disorder"
The Fem, "tantrum"; "slasher"
Gigantic Sequins, "tenderling"
glitterMOB, "hurting to ask you"
Grimoire, "wooded ephemeral"; "abacus"
Hobart, "glistering"; "ouch"
Luna Luna, "split oak"
Magic Jar, "thumbelina sleepwalk"
MISTRESS, "lachrymose"
Moonsick Magazine, "tincture"; "torn"; "unrequited"
Noble / Gas Qtrly, "abecedarian with sexual tension"; "phantasm"; "reverie"
Quail Bell Magazine, "marionette"; "morose" "smolder"
Rogue Agent, "concoction"
Rust + Moth, "girl/creature"; "stoking the embers"
Sea Foam Mag, "gutshot"; "growl"
Tinderbox Poetry Journal, "stricken"; "humble creatures"
velvet-tail, "twang"
Winter Tangerine, "girl/costume"; "wintering"
Word Riot, "bestiary"

Brain Mill Press, "pretty pretty princess vs. the underworld" included in chapbook *My Tall Handsome*

Platypus Press, "hex"; "covet"; "silhouette"; "contaminant"; "trellis" included in chapbook *darkling*

"stoking the embers" alludes to a line from the fairy tale *Cinderella* by the Brothers Grimm (1812): There's blood in the shoe. The shoe is too tight, This bride is not right!

"thumbelina sleepwalk" alludes to lyrics from the song "Thumbelina," featured in Don Bluth's animated adaptation *Thumbelina* (1994).

Inspired by Laura Theobald's *The Best Thing Ever*, the poems in "hurting to ask you" were initially composed using predicative text software on a Samsung Galaxy S4 Mini, and were revised separately, not relying exclusively on the word choices provided by the predictive software.

"tenderling" takes after the form in Emily O'Neill's poem "Need to Know"

"trellis" was inspired by the poet, Gwen Werner.

tenderling

teηderling
Copyright © 2017 By Emily Corwin
ISBN: 978-0-9991152-1-3
Library Of Congress data available on request.

First paperback edition published by Stalking Horse Press, February 2018

All rights reserved. Except for brief passages quoted for review or academic purposes, no part of this book may be reproduced, stored in a retrieval system, or transmitted by any means without the written permission of the author and publisher. Published in the United States by Stalking Horse Press.

The characters and events in this book are fictitious or used fictitiously. Any similarity to real persons, living or dead, is coincidental and not intended by the author.

www.stalkinghorsepress.com

Design by James Reich
Cover Illustration by Sarah Shields
www.saraheshields.com

Stalking Horse Press
Santa Fe, New Mexico

Stalking Horse Press requests that authors designate a nonprofit, charitable, or humanitarian organization to receive a portion of revenue from the sales of each title.

emily corwin

tenderling

STALKING HORSE PRESS
SANTA FE, NEW MEXICO

table of contents

hex - 13
tincture - 14
tantrum - 15
reverie - 16
girl/creature - 17
bestiary - 18
thumbelina sleepwalk - 21
split oak - 22
torn - 23
contaminant - 24
smolder - 25
abecedarian with sexual tension - 26
lachrymose - 28
pretty pretty princess vs. the underworld - 29
twang - 38
phantasm - 39
girl/costume - 40
gutshot - 41
growl - 42
slasher - 43

table of contents (cont.)

wintering - 44
apparition - 45
wooded ephemeral - 46
abacus - 47
anxiety disorder - 48
marionette - 49
glistering - 50
silhouette - 51
morose - 52
briars - 53
hurting to ask you - 54
thirsty - 56
tongue scraper - 57
covet - 58
concoction - 59
let me hold myself - 60
stricken - 61
unrequited - 62
tenderling - 63
trellis - 64

For Joe and Soup

tenderling

hex

if I go under wood, a girl darkling for curse, for
meat white, for thistle and sting. if I am brave. if I
bury all my dead parts. if the house melts over my
bread slice. if strawberry, if the hunter's knife
glides in and out. if I am made a stone, if I
nightmare, bolting on every ground.

tincture

here is my blouse, emptied. white eyelet,
blood-let—red stain becomes brown stain
becomes evidence. here, a throat soured,
a hole plugged with taffeta. here, muscle
tissue. here, peeled open with sugar ants.
I am as naked as I could be—just marrow,
dead leaf in my chest. here, bitter. here,
hollowed. I make trouble, rustling the cold
wild. if you step in me, I won't forgive. I
ruin, I hurt—here and here and here, you
turn see-through, crystalline, a shape
gliding over soil.

tantrum

at first, this terrible mirror, gutted. it is thinking of taking me.
at midnight, screaming illness, I fill a particular dark. I rustle, I
thrash—a girl loose in the bramble, getting wretched, smashing
up a glass syringe. how to return this rage, how it circles endless
—like bruise, like stone too black. I get hurt in you, becoming
skeleton. my ruffles everywhere, wilting.

reverie

I ate the honeycomb whole and now there are bees inside me. a leaf drips out of my underwear; I try to look human today. my panic—unrelenting, my ball -gown gone missing, somewhere under the blossoms. in the nights, I return to him often, to the place where slept our bodies, young and peaceful, and I wonder if he also returns, if we happen to meet, if he would kiss me a little in the closets—touch like mercy, like a long -awaited relief. we lay down our breadknives, we lay ourselves down in quiet, feeling our way toward a sweetness, toward my insides humming.

girl/creature

she wakes   rise and shine
in the queen anne's lace

    girl in lingerie and choke-cherries
    girl silky for touches   in the meadow
    her antlers budding velvet

        no four-chambered heart
        just an heirloom tomato.

girl with a bellyache—thorn stuck
above her pubic bone
        she didn't go down easy

    girl with a pretty mouth hole—she ought to run now
        from the bad thing lurking   run into the bark moss
            milkweed and screech

she best be on her way
    hurry up now, sweetie
        pack up your money, your hard bread

    the meadow rustling, awake
    girl with a home to get home to
    before the day's dark   girl with a head start
        tomato heart aflutter.

bestiary

i.

say: I want to be smothered to be wrecked and mouthwatering
    a crushed party dress, creamy   say: I want bling and dusty rose
polyester   slipper and hustle   I want matrimony   in a pasture, darkly
cornflower swirly curly up my ankles   say: water the mouth
                                      the mouth is watering.

ii.

I'm crushing on this guy   he's totally amaze
smooches me   smackers all over   say: I want to be smothered
    say: water the mouth   water the roots
        he's like the perfect dude   fine as hell and devil forks.
        he shakes my hemoglobin up   I'm his flesh trophy   this is matrimony.

    we come together wham—   a bundle of cedar wood and shampoo
                        espresso   hammers and wild mint
                black orchid   and lotions   tea leaves
                noodles   and cuff links   and mulled wine
                    doves   cherries   totems.
      say: I want this wreck, my mouth still watering.

iii.

we were young & hungry   we were dressed to kill
    the big bad wolves, smokin in their zoot suits   tobacco snuff and teeth.
say: let's take these suckers down   let's wear red capes and squabble
        leave the tux, take the shotgun holler   fur looks so good on you.

iv.

into the gooey   the mucky bogs and maple root   say: water the mouth
    the mouth is watering   say: here is a little dipper   a little grub and drink
let's get smashed, baby cake   my dress rumpled, creamy   bewitch me
    say: we can smother one another   we two we honeymooners   in a pasture, darkly.

v.

when the witchy came   with her crooked hair crimp and rags
                    with her forked tongue   supple

she came around and I was all like: *hey what's a witchy like you doing in my woods?*
    and then she's all like: *take it easy, girlie   take a bite of this magic bean*
                    you look a little rawboned, a little ravenous

when I suckle it down   magic bean delight   my body withers
    shrunk down to a sprout I am teensy weensy   —a thumbelina, naked.
say: I want to be smothered my party dress, creamy, it smothers me
                      crushed into a white ocean, taffeta.

the witchy, she snickers   with her chai tea fingers cloves   frankincense
    she goes after my man   he's like the perfect dude
she likes that cornflower swirly curly up his ankles   fine as hell and devil forks
    say: water the mouth   her mouth turns watery.

vi.

didn't take to her charms   horoscopes and stones   bad potion
                    it didn't taste right to him

the witchy, she scorned   she spit some omens out
    a mean broth—   his body withers   shrunk to a mucus green

                a *ribbit ribbit* and croak   say: I want to be wrecked
say: in a pasture, darkly   bewitch me   we two, we bottomfeeders
                            woodsy creatures   astonished and wet.

vii.

I grow babies on my backside   tadpoles, squiggle and gel
   we made the best of things   we made a home of sticks and watercress.
     I am teensy weensy   —a thumbelina
      he is amphibian, sleek husband in the pasture, darkly

this is matrimony. I want swamp lily and aloe   ragweed
               fluids, rough and teeming   I want earthy and succulent

                       say: I want to be smothered   I want to be wrecked—
                  a crushed party dress a flesh trophy   a thumbelina
                                      mouth that waters, yearning.

thumbelina sleepwalk

out there, there is the big, big world
    there is full of sparrows and tadpoles and mole holes.

        she watches, girl no bigger than a bumble bee
            girl long ago with wings she plucked them off

                now blisters, now restless in her walnut shell
                    at the window ledge—a moonstuck place

                    her face—a pretty penny against the glass
                    eyes beady, all kindle and shine.

split oak

you felt me, you left me—moaning open in a landslide. I harden like grease and there's glimmer. the saplings anxious for ripping, cleaved the way you like it. let's say: you're the woodsman and I am a girl, slipping in a magician box, my bra cups filling out—buttermilk, tiny bow in the middle. you wield a saw, a tremor—sung like choirs, biting through.

torn

how it goes: white leather, red leather, mammal—at the center, sweet embryo. how you went clawing through, how I forked you out. how I *run run run* like shadow rabbit on wall. how I make house: spittle, grain, gather up this field blissful, field raging. how you can't spell slaughter without laughter. how I make you stay, my dearest—in a canning jar, in hickory, in cider, salt oozing. how I go howling never, how I look at you, so dragged through and rough.

contaminant

now, I lift upward the edges of this garment—soft-hearted, bowl into which I stock the winter apples. now, the muscle of me uncoils over rye grass. now, I want something not wrong, asking aloud if I am still kind, gracious—if I am still your girl. when I am inside this absolute and ringing terror, I turn back to my mother, she feels, oh my mother, she knows in a past life she went breathing as a horse —rump, hock, heart-girth in the valley. I am not good like that. more like, I think, like a river beast, maw-full, now with silt, bloodworm, cruelty.

smolder

ever I felt things in these rooms—a handful of tinder sticks, listen for sputter. becoming milkweed, becoming a wick gone crispy, a bride come back to the party and all the guests are elsewhere. I miss everybody, but leave me alone for goodness sake, why don't you, don't you go tumbling in the lake rust— decay is what you're smelling, a sunken dress—bleached, open husk, arms raised in shimmer.

abecedarian with sexual tension

are you running to someplace that
beckons you? in the wild yonder, where I

crackle, the lungs of me blooming silver in the
dimness, riverbed gone out. should we meet then at

evening? under coxcomb and swollen,
filled with asking for each other, asking whether

goodness can be taught, whether this is right. and
how do you heal yourself, my dear?

I remember what you are—scab, totem,
juniper on the side of this house. do you make me

kind? would you like to reach between my doors—
lurid as a milksnake? I break every promise

made once to myself, in the darkening, dark
now, and my blackberries are burnt. I put fire

on the table, the rosewood made soft and
pinkish. I long to be among your

quiet plants, your neck unclothed, your wrist and
rhubarb, the red thorny vine coiling,

smoked in you—a heat that pulls, dragging anyone
toward it, toward being raptured,

unmade by your finger tips, undone my ribs,
vertebrae—scraped, used like a

whetstone. it is scary, to live like this, under the
x-ray machines, everything visible in my

young chest—a threshold. enter me between a
zillion bright rooms, all at once hushing.

lachrymose

oh my god I am over the mobile data limit. oh my god serotonin reuptake inhibitor. oh my god spine brightening in the strawberry field. my god I lay deep everywhere ever. my god take me to your mansion now. my god a woman messages me to say that I seem "sweet" and would I like "some extra cash for school or vacation?" my god I want a floret growing rapid from my every orifice. my goodness you know how much I love him. my goodness there are men outside my home with power tools. my goodness all of my life I thought the expression: "it was a scorcher out there today" was really: "it was a scorchard out there today"—like an orchard set aflame, the pulp crisping ashen. my goodness me the emotional torment. my goodness me this millennium. good gracious me this pesticide, dirty chai, cat skull, cake wife, eye gunk, homicide. good gracious me how are you, little bean? good gracious I remove the plump oil pores from me like surgery. good gracious as a girl, I came home declaring that in the movie, "Bambi's mommy got dead." oh my good graces I am noxious as climbing nightshade. oh my god my body in affliction, in affection. oh my god you can't vanish on me now, into the ether, chilling my optical nerve and nerve cords, discordant. oh my god this microbe that takes me, ferments into an awful dread. my god the world is not doing so very well. my god I want to eat noodles and stay awake. my god this dark music awaiting.

pretty pretty princess vs. the underworld

i.

my tall handsome, you are always
hydrangea in my rib, popped open
always dazzle of salt on my punched lip

love of life
the he & me I will devour

we beneath black cherry tree
all fruits and crystals on your chest

you were my first body—now and always
forever and ever, in the pink bed rippling
                                            amen.

ii.

Being with you is heavenly, really
heavenly in the pearly slipper night

        twirling, twirling up that cocktail rum & coke magic
                that hocus pocus ballroom twinkle
                        that witching hour with a long red kiss

my tall handsome and me, we gonna get hitched
   my arms pinched in beads brocade teardrop tiaras

I walk in a chiffon mermaid spell
I walk in the room with a white swan glued against my back

      girl in the moon with the glitter tongue ravaging
     I sip the goblet down, tip it upside down, wear it as a hat

  I am a new shiny thing
    and I steal you away from the hoopla hullabaloo rumpus
              to a stardust garden   I drip grapes into your perfect mouth

bite your chest find paradise   my sugar boo, my muffin cake

my tall handsome—always hydrangea and dazzle of salt
       always my popped rib and punched lip milky
       always fruits and crystals, the black cherry tree shaking

iii.

into the orchard, into the crabapple abracadabra
              we snap a sugarplum, slap the guts into our gums
                            pulp so yellow sloppy

     I am perfectly hideous, you are perfectly hunky
    forever and ever in a stardust disaster   amen

scoop me up, my tall handsome
      take your bride, your one beloved
             to the glass coffin, to the pink bed rippling

              a snow pea stuck in the mattress
    bow down to your nit-picky finicky fussy little princess

I stay up forever, can't zzzzzzz   zzzzzzz   zzzzzzzzzzzzzz
    I chase your heartbeat pitter patter
        it goes skip skippety like baby rabbit fluff
                     a rifle cracking the robin egg blue

you were my first body
       the pink bed ripples.

               I strike up the candlestick and the smoke so mystical
               I giddy up, whipping a carousel horse across your absence

your shut-eye golden goldenrod
       like dandelion wine and buttermilk hot cakes mango honey yummm

the he & me I will devour

iv.

tulips   two lips   two ripples shake the pink sheet

the he & me, two cherries smooshed in a pie
       two peas in a mattress
       two itty bitty glitter tongues ravaging

my tall handsome in the tallest tower
              in the bedroom ripe with flames
              and nightingales

            lingerie
                   caterpillars
                             rubies
                   scones   lavender and dead bees
    and cappuccinos   soaps
                             and puppet strings   bells
  ripening with valentines   oils   alphabet
                     coins   and ghosts
          pink wine   shadowboxes
    cough drops   witch hazel   white swan
            sequins   lightning

       bedroom ripe with pomegranate   goblets

                                                      ribbon

           dazzle of salt   rum & coke magic
                 paradise

       hydrangea

v.

in the tallest tower
         in a chiffon mermaid spell   I sex you up
                                   snow peas ripple on the pink bed
I devour you, sugar boo
you were my first body, muffin cake

         now and always, my hunky man candy
                    so hot, I could bake cookies on you

    I could eat you right up   all salt dazzle butterstick oatmeal spoon
                              those fruits and crystals on your chest

we beneath black cherry tree
         with punched lips drunk hands glitter tongues ravaging ravaging
         we cuddle buddy, we snooze off into the sunset
                 forever and ever   tall handsome snookums beloved amen.

vi.

I miss you
  misplace you
         I lose you already

    my tall handsome   under the black cherry tree, shaking
          the wood sizzles with clocks rivers trumpets ropes
                      the wood splits apart, gutted

      and the underworld swooshes up
      underworld feasting on your heartbeat pitter patter
          your gorgeous mouth, perfect hunky
              your fruits and crystals
              your long red kiss

      I miss you   misplace you   I lose you already

vii.

into the pit   into the black cherry tree, gutted
      you vanish, radiant   somersault into the wet chanting abyss

and I am undone   darling   sugar cake.
                          I saw the black robe shrieking

I saw the one with the mirror cheek rattling wicked wicked

I saw him with daggers   rowboats   hooks   volcanoes

   I saw him jingle jangle there

      I saw him drag your heart across the wood

   you dash away   into the cherry tree
   you tall handsome corpse you
   dash away dash away   forever and ever in a stardust disaster

And I am undone. I am all tiaras lingerie glitter tongue smashed
                                      across your absence

        hydrangea glowing in my diaphragm, punched lip milky

viii.

with my pearly slipper
        with rum & coke magic
        and snow peas and a chiffon mermaid
                with my pretty princess hair

        I saddle up my carousel horse and gallop
                into the wet chanting abyss
                into the wood that sizzles and shakes

I'm crashing right behind you, darling
        into the pit swarmed with clocks and trumpets choked red eyes

        clip clop I go to where the black robe shrieks
        where his mirror cheek rattles   wicked   wicked
                                    across your absence

I see you rippling   in a perfect black hole
                    what a bright gorgeous swirl you are

    I chase your heartbeat pitter patter
        I whiplash the glass pony and giddy up fast
                prancing into the void

                            the void ripe with flames
                            and bullets
                  ginger
                      chemicals
                jellyfish
            and rosehips
                    and gasoline

                salamander
                needles   pepper
                        mosquito bites
                and gargoyle
                and dinosaurs

        the void ripe with trumpets
                        and numbers
                                pitchfork
            hooks
                    volcano

            ripe with fruits and crystals
            on your chest   my tall handsome

ix.

At the end of the black hole
in the wet abyss chanting, there is a chair.
And in that chair, there is a robe.
And in that robe, there is a wicked wicked cheek that is a mirror

    he churns above me, that shrieking man
    he jingle jangles, he rattles when I gallop into the room

and you are there—gorgeous buttercup shimmer you are

    I want you back, sugar boo
      the black robe shrieks bloody murder

        I lay down my peace offerings—slipper, snow pea, grapes, teardrop tiara
                          also hot cakes
                          also tulips
                          and candlestick

                    and smoke so mystical
                    and hocus pocus ballroom twinkle

    his cheek rattling always wicked always ravaging, insatiable

        so I lay me down
        my pretty princess hair
        my glitter tongue and white swan glued against my back

the black robe jingle jangles
                he cuts me up with hooks and choked red eyes
                girl in the moon—I am a shiny new thing
                I am willing to be gutted

        he picks the tasty precious bits
                an eye
                      a tooth
                          an ovary

    I will devour you
    slurps it all into his gullet so wicked so spittle drip jugular
                                        ever shrieking

x.

you were my first body
and your body comes back to me amen
my tall handsome with fruits and crystals glinting splendorous baby cake
being with you is heavenly sugar boo

I am perfectly hideous, you are perfectly hunky
        I am a hot mess   gutted little ruin

and still you pucker up
and still you clutch my gruesome face

        you mack all over me
        and it's a sparkler spell-breaking cherry bomb kinda kiss, amen

we blast out of the underworld
past chemicals   gasoline   salamander   trumpets

the black robe grinning wicked rattles   a farewell shriek and we shoot back   smack dab

into the orchard
     to the crabapple abracadabra
   in the tallest tower
   the pink sheet rippling

I laugh merrily into your neck
my punched lip, my one eye weeping paradise amen
I am lovey dovey jubilee   forever and ever darling
you are my tall handsome, my sugar boo zombie man
and I—your broken sugarplum

love of life
    the he & me I will devour
                forever and ever
                    in the pink bed
                    in a chiffon mermaid spell
                    in my rib, popped open
                    tall handsome
                    beloved
                    into the sunset
                    amen
                    amen
                    amen
                    hydrangea.

twang

with all my hearts, with a sparking against the witchgrass, my witch dress swish swish. remember to remember my voice under the neck, my collapse into spidersilk, velvet-leaf. I come back to this confused room, memory of tendons, nervous to be felt.

phantasm

branches all over and I'm calling you forth:
you kindred one, you bent low in the hazel.
what am I allowed to want? under the barn
gleamed hunger, the eyeholes shiver there.

    spirit that's kindred, spirit that's kind, bent like
    a witch hazel. what if the body decides to keep
    you? so hungered for gristle, black lumber, eyelet.
    brought down with symptom, you break my hair

        now. and what does the body keep? the
        hayfields, oats, a reckoning like high fever
        and my hair is alight with kerosene, riven.
        I carry muscle and a little basket. my field

            of visions, I reckon every illness. what are
            we allowed, under the barn—thriving nerve,
            a basket silent with kindling, lightwood, the
            branches against us, spirit calling me over.

girl/costume

I am sewn into the dress
    crinoline is rough and scratch.

    I have a pretty room with a pretty rocking horse
    and hairbrush and ribbons hoopskirt
    the wedding silver and grime.

        girl, hands folded girl with aching
                daylight burnt in the attic.

I want so badly to give you body
    hot-blooded, tender   running fevers

    running across the barley fields
    until femur bone pokes through
                to be sick for you

        shivering like candlewicks
        every tip and fiber lighted.

gutshot

too much bruise out of
nowhere, too much my
body hurting my body.
too much nightmare in
the night. too much your
hands, too much I quake.
at sundown, at the edge
of scorching, too much
like kerosene, too much
I become a puncture for
mending.

growl

I walk uphill, frightening myself with sequins, with shrieking—
I chase after, scissors and glisten. whenever my hunger, when it
takes me, I eat—one tablet by mouth and the hills go *shhhhh* and
homeward, how I rattle, split underneath—a cutlet soaking for
the butcher.

slasher

a lot of me comes out: pulp, cherry syrup, clot in the skirt.
he says, *it's like a crime scene down there*. I drip over the
grasses. at dusk, I climb inside a beaded purse, to get safe.
I fold into a wet dot, oily, rumpled in the creases. he stands
over me with weapons, with appetite, with a horse bridle
and bowls of disinfectant, makes me a sanitary girl.

wintering

impossible to keep warm like this—in my sheerest form, membrane-like and white as a sheet, two holes for eyes and hands lifting up, up. I am faint of heart, dear one. nothing to eat but twigs out here. what I would give for solid foods and you, sweetheart, your heart so sweet, I am lusty for it. this girl delicate, flimsy—a cobweb, this girl always dressed by furry woodland creatures. girl looking for a village, a bowl of mush and beans, a marriage vow. what I would give for something hearty, to last the year and then some.

apparition

blackthorn runs beneath me like a beautiful flake of mirror, crushed. I have been in the ground, seen the warm milk from a shadow. when it was after dark, my eyes shone like insects—horrific, moving too much. I wear this gown beneath the lake—dirty molecule, popped seam, gossamer—in the membrane there, I almost become a human being, fleshy as a rosette, drowned. I loved you with all of my soul, loved you young & thriving in the oxygen. where will you go beyond me? I want the bloodstream a little longer, to be warm-hearted, touchable everywhere.

wooded ephemeral

alone with you in a phone call, on this fallen planet,
broken meadow I make aglow like bruise—a loud

contusion. when it comes to you & I—embracing, magnetic,
almost in danger—I cannot even, cannot think. like an

evergreen in the middle of anywhere, the trunk axed, I always
flinch at you. my scabs leak & become brittle. between us—a

glitch, error message, a sugar. I think you are so honey,
honeycrisp as the apples in my cheeks, skin I try to make more

illumined, radiant for the party. do you like this cocktail dress?
jacquard, rhinestone, ruched—one that I could wear for the occasion,

kissing you under the bower. I would like to keep you sheltered, warmly
like a spore. don't go away over the phone. I need support & service for

my feelings, need ravishing now more than ever, geraniums
now more than ever, something soft & redolent to

obsess you, to catch your heart over. I collect the green needles, the
pines are molting. I feel molten like a fragment of coal fire, so

quickly scattered there in the soil, the particulate brown & saturated.
remember the not-so-long ago—this wilted corset, this corsage

tight, once erotic to me. you live now only in the messages, digital—
until some future hour to make ours, thrashing together

wherever insects are abundant, two maws sucking out the
xylem vessels from the leaves, rucking our good clothing.

you have such a beautiful skull in there—I long to peel you back, unzipper
these body glands, warm my hands in your liquid, dazzling.

abacus

I use my phone as a mirror. I have zero likes. I like
mud-rose & jewelweed & you. you left my body cells

astonished. I am missing you something fierce in these
greenfields & oil fields & fields of scary love I do not like.

such a long way from this little while together. with you,
it is a presence or absence of claws—your hands that might

injure. desire holds me like a knife. *what do you want me to
say to that?* you say back. I research what larger animals are

most likely to kill me in the surrounding areas—most likely
horse or dog—& you think my hair is alive & it is. I get so

impossible with emotion, blighted, startled like a starling.
I order the latest version of a cave—tight, dripping—where

I can disappear into. I remember we enjoyed getting down
low in the bull thistle, downloading each other. you sent:

remember this? in your message request. the attachment
failed to load, inside the glow screen, silken.

anxiety disorder

I guess someone is having a party somewhere—my gowns, how
they racket, wanting to float intimate against me. first night with

a prozac capsule and there is wolf spider in my stomach, another
spiraled behind my eyesight. I would like to be happy at night,

when it is cold by the window, cold under the nail cuticles. *be
nourished and mighty!* says the whole foods commercial, and I

look at my reflecting image, at the fat stores, rumpled. do not take
my skin away—why do you sharpen your carbon steel knives? for

hours, I writhe like a half-dead carcass, clicking my mouthparts,
obsessed, apprehensive that everybody hates me, hated me, will

hate me in the imminent future. what I do best is worry—
silent and injured, a succubus on my abdomen glutting itself.

marionette

my sundress—black cherry, drenched. tonight, I am caked, I spit —brown sugar, autumn mums I reaped. throwing a hiss, throwing spite around like a boiled nectar, how will I will myself out? they took my bad things happening—they pulled out every girl, filling a vial. all season long, I break my closest things. I guess home is always a place I have slept in. I guess you want me—whittled down, pretty as a cobbler.

glistering

back there—just ugly things I don't want to look at.
my thirst sitting under your hand, almost disappeared.
I move like infection, gleaming, rushing across—a girl
like tallow candle in the room. in dark cedars, in night
terror, I spread quickly, pray the ground shining up.

silhouette

the glass flares, then goes out black, lightning will lighten
my surfaces. I am preparing for the cold season, carving an
arrow, my own red tendon for bow string, rigid for the kill.
to survive means forget, means to misremember, dismember
the old shadow room. *don't make me live without*—I speak
to no one in particular.

morose

what's a girl to do with this hoofed animal, when it brings
her, when it splinters and she is swallowed up in the road—
softest tendril, the blackbirds closing in. she wanted to live
her life as someone—a girl gripping mirrors, dark sometimes.
sometimes awaiting, under maples and gloom, some bit of
sweetness crawling out.

briars

there was a boy in my room and it's secret. I would like to
return my body now. would you like to come into, come and
see? me with my clothing with the roses, thistle, barb. lots of
dread, lots of asking permission. he says how well things are
going and I am glad, glad he is well, that he is doing so very
well now, maybe we should have been broke like that. the urge
to say: *do you feel safe where you are?* to say: *I don't believe
you've done the things you've done to me.* how one day, I leapt,
big-hearted, after into the rupture—
it was my body they pulled out.

hurting to ask you
after Laura Theobald

hey, you are my best place for winter.
I was not sure you wanted me back there.
there is rust and wanting you. I missed the
deadline for the dark. I turn myself out.
*

we have the right place to stay in touch. so look forward
to hearing from the year before. I have been in hospitals
for you. come here as a friend of mine. I am ready.
I have a heart of gold and silverware.
*

hey honey, tell me how to make do without
breaking up the road please. the world like
a good place for sale. are you doing this for
the first time in forever? are you coming
to find out
*

how are things with me? I am using the latest version of myself.
you are not the intended recipient, you get me wrong with loads
of worship. I think it would be best if I kept the romantic dinner.
*

I don't know what it is I am supposed to
connect to. please remember to send my
errands. we are going to the party room for
a little bit more and then the upcoming disaster
at a theater near you, the address listed below.
*

you are my rock and house, thank goodness.
I am sorry for not getting back to the room
in the morning. I have been thinking about
your asking for the end, the end of time and
money to pay for it.
*

my throat hurting to ask you
a little gloomy here. I am
available for purchase.
*

I fell asleep for the weekend
in the home of your old life.
it was such a thing of days ago.
I want to apologize again—
my darling, don't think that I
can make it.
*

thirsty

my god, the lightshine dapples you like the backside
of a living thing. my god, you keep me woken, nervous
girl in the crocus, impossible for rest. wanting to willfully
cut off your arms in the clearing, there with yarrow and
ancient flood, my god, with your last calling across: *why
are you still doing this; I was never yours at all.*

tongue scraper

infested overnight, my body holes turned petri dish—mildew, creatures, a filth streaked across. I am looking forward to thunderstorm, severe darkness for the rest of this century, for this banquet, spoilt in a warm, black place. ask if I am better now—no longer that girl embittered, no longer swelling under softwood flooring. I promise you, I pinky swear, you won't like it—what comes now, rotted, out of mouth.

covêt

this old room and shadow, coming home now the dark falls down me—neckhole, clavicle, underwear and touch. in you, I always feel hospitalized, sweetened like crystals. I have rubbed myself all over your garden—velvet leaf, milkwood. did you know that I am really into sugar right now? maybe like shortbread, maybe like a screech and madness, like doll blood, doll in a pale sheet, cords tied at the back.

concoction

I surfaced from the pot like a bobbing apple, a first squishy vertebrate. the afterbirth ladled into goblets—tart sip, vinegar. they swaddled me up —cheesecloth over my nubs, tentacles flinching in a dry world. and so I was made, pickled with the best ingredients and brought writhing into the crust. they prepared for me a crib, a sugar cube, a pocket mirror in which to study myself—fine specimen—to watch the big show as I turned into pink, into legs and breast tissue, still thirsty—limbs basting in the tub.

let me hold myself

the old church dress doesn't fit me in the chest. I misread the hours. seeking advice on matters of money & the heart. I decide I like the bramble vodka & the other drinks have names like nectar & night huntress. how much is it, do you know? do you know what it means to be infected? rot, fevers, outburst, need for touching in the quarantine. too much in my system, I get so ruthless with my own well-being. don't go soft on this now, do not become howling in the dressing room, do not yield, like thaw, like forgotten produce in the cupboards. take up that axe, break me in case of fire.

stricken

I know you will know what I mean—that I am meant for you, back in the alcoves, you come thudding in the nightfall and I am fallen, felled like a poplar in the heartland, yes. back there are the trees, yes. I carry the eyebright on my back, yes, among all this bacteria and loam. I am never able to keep someone. and already in my side—a long spoke piercing, a slash liquid—something to lay your hands into.

unrequited

however this old river, however it greens. however with a hatchet, with a gown of heavy whipping cream. how things bloom outward, onward, ripened for my picking. how I came from the branches, tiny gashes all over. how often, I turn brittle, to be snapped across your knee. however I hunt you, how I squint behind thorn-dark, cracked open like sproutling, like fruit rot—perishable, craving to be sucked.

tenderling

i.

in a bad goodnight, in a good stove blackening,
I am a girl of pony hair—a bagful of ribbon. when
I dress the wounds, when I dress myself with figs
and coffee berries, and I get very emotional about
you. I care so very much, I just want to know you
are good and alive—here at day break, broken.

ii.

the day breaks, it is broken like cups. you are alive
and good, I awaken as if hit over the head with a soft,
gentle hammer. I hurry along the country, bringing
rhubarb and a branch, dark and oaken in my mouth—
an offering, something to place against your ugly door
—my love, my once darling. for you, I am catching
cold, catching hold of this glittering.

iii.

I catch coldness here, I hold the glitter. can we agree
to forget this? forget last night with my cocktail, my
caring so much for so little in my hand? today, I awaken
with burn, a light-rush, a stove going black. you say
where I am is a place you could never love, could never
be alive in. too much cornsilk, too much gaping like
a skinned deer baby—too much, I am too much.

iv.

too much, I am a baby deer for skinning—girl hurting in the
corn, pony hair and ribbons. forget the rhubarb, the branch dark
and oaken. forget my emotion—caring too much for your ugly
door. I dress in figs, the stove blackens to coals, and love that
you are, once darling, in the worst goodbye, I am a girl—
alive, at day breaking open.

trellis

a thorn in my side—I put it there. I ruin my
own days, keep strange hours. call me american
honey, but stale. don't put me in your cupboard,
don't put me in your tea leaves foreboding towards
catastrophe. I am not as good as I believed—always
falling, failing, collapse—a spill of birds, a girl ripened
with dead gardens.

about emily corwin

Emily Corwin is an MFA candidate in poetry at Indiana University-Bloomington and the former Poetry Editor for *Indiana Review*. Her writing has appeared or is forthcoming in *Gigantic Sequins, Day One, Hobart, Yemassee, THRUSH*, and elsewhere. She has two chapbooks, *My Tall Handsome* (Brain Mill Press) and *darkling* (Platypus Press) which were published in 2016.

You can follow her online at @exitlessblue.

www.ingramcontent.com/pod-product-compliance
Lightning Source LLC
Chambersburg PA
CBHW020625300426
44113CB00007B/777